ST ALBANS CATHEDRAL

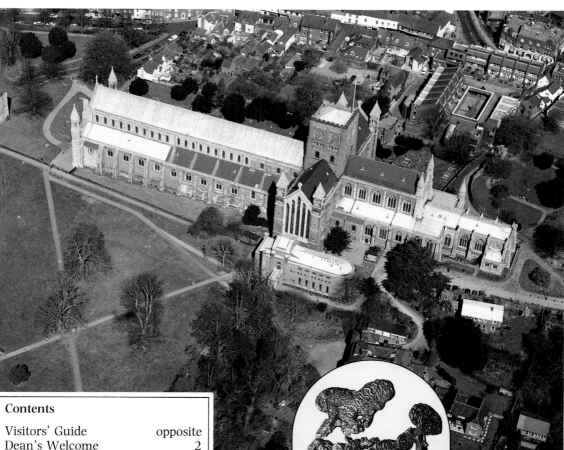

Contents

Visitors' Guide	opposite
Dean's Welcome	2
History Chart	3
The Story of Alban	4
The Changing Face of the Nave	6
Great Days of the Monastery	8
Dissolution	10
The Transepts	12
The Tower and Presbytery	16
The Chapel of St Alban	18
The Lady Chapel	20
Victorian Restoration	22
The Lords go to Law	24
The Chapter House	26
The Church Today	28

Above:
The Cathedral and Abbey Church of St Alban – the heart of the city on a hill.

Left:
A 14th-century pilgrim badge from the Verulamium Museum showing the martyrdom of St Alban; a rare survival.

Dean's Welcome

This is the Cathedral and Abbey Church of St Alban and it is unique in having that description. I hope your interest in the abbey will be whetted by this beautiful publication. You will also learn a lot about the thousand years of worship which have continued here on the site of Alban's martyrdom. The shrine, which has been recently restored, still stands at the east end of the church.

Many centuries ago Alban was the first Christian martyr in this country and his shrine has always attracted pilgrims in search of spiritual and physical healing. Now you are here too, and I hope that you will feel God's power in this place where a brave man died for his faith. Stay as long as you can, and you will surely go on your way refreshed in body and spirit.

History Chart

Early 3rd century:
Martyrdom of Alban.

793 King Offa endowed the monastery.

1077 Paul de Caen appointed Abbot: Roman tiles used to build the Norman church.

1154 Nicholas Breakspear appointed Pope Adrian IV.

1200 John de Cella rebuilt west end.

1213 Meeting of barons which led to Magna Carta in 1215.

1320 New east end completed.

1323 South arcade collapsed.

1400 Watching loft installed.

1447 Duke of Gloucester's Chapel built.

1484 High altar screen erected.

1520 Ramryge chantry built.

1539 Dissolution of the monastery.

1553 Church bought by townspeople. Lady Chapel became a school.

1832 Restoration began.

1856 Sir George Gilbert Scott appointed architect.

1862 Nave murals uncovered.

1870 Lady Chapel reverted to church use. Tower strengthened. Shrine pedestal restored.

1877 Church became a cathedral.

1880 Lord Grimthorpe obtained Faculty for restoration.

1982 New Chapter House opened.

1989 Laporte window unveiled.

A south-west view of the abbey in 1800.

The Story of Alban

Alban was a citizen of Verulamium, one of the most important Roman towns in the country. The historian Bede wrote that Alban, a pagan, received and sheltered in his house a fugitive from persecution. The sight of the stranger's constant prayers and vigils impressed Alban, who sought instruction from him. Alban accepted the Christian faith and disguised his visitor, later known as Amphibalus, in his own distinctive cloak to enable him to escape. Alban was brought before the town magistrates, where he refused to acknowledge the pagan gods of Rome, saying 'I worship and adore the true and living God.' Christianity was a proscribed religion in the Roman Empire and Alban was accordingly condemned to death. He was taken from the city to the hillside, and was executed where the church now stands – thus in *c.* AD 209 becoming the first Christian martyr in this country.

A reputation for miracles of healing at the site of the martyrdom attracted an increasing number of pilgrims. By 429 St Germanus of Auxerre visited a shrine here, where to this day there has been continuous Christian worship. Early in the 8th century Bede wrote of the 'beautiful Church worthy of Alban's martyrdom where frequent miracles of healing took place.' This church had a monastic structure which was reordered by King Offa of Mercia in 793. He established the Rule of St Benedict in a double monastery which he richly endowed. The Saxon buildings would have been of typical timber-framed construction. In the 960s, in the reign of King Edgar, St Oswald brought new order and discipline to many Benedictine houses throughout the land, including St Albans. Later abbots collected building materials from the long-abandoned Roman town of Verulamium, intending a reconstruction of the abbey church. Difficult times were made worse by Viking invasions so the

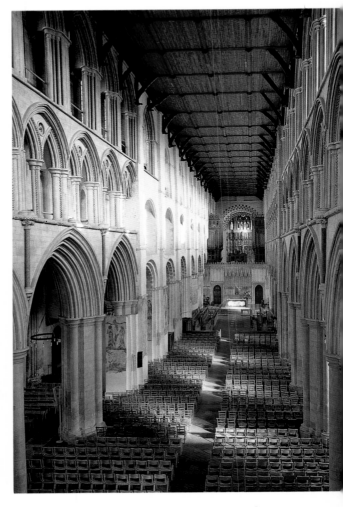

Above:
The nave looking east, showing the rich variety of architecture and decoration: Norman, Early English and Decorated.

work was never started.

The stock of material which the Saxon abbots had accumulated proved invaluable when the Normans came in 1066. Yet the conquerors, although Christian, regarded the Saxons as *rudes et idiota* and were determined to show their own superiority. Here was the opportunity to build bigger and better than anything local people had ever seen and, with materials to hand, a start was made in 1077 on a huge Norman church. The grand conception and design would have

I worship and adore the True and Living God who created all things.'

THE PRAYER OF ST ALBAN.

Right:
Matthew Paris (d.1259), chronicler of the abbey, wrote and illustrated the *Historia Anglorum*. Here is his self-portrait, kneeling before the Virgin and Child.

...een created by the new masters but it should be remembered that most of the skills were those practised by Saxon workmen. The first Norman Abbot, Paul ...e Caen, brought Robert from Normandy ...s master mason, whom he described as *...nirabilis magister'*. Robert worked here ...ntil his death in 1114.

Paul was Italian by birth, a kinsman ...f Lanfranc, Archbishop of Canterbury, ...ho encouraged the cult of the saints ...nd the building of huge churches. ...Vhen the church was dedicated in 1115 ... was the largest in England. It was ...evere and strong. The Roman bricks ...vere too hard to be carved so the round-...opped arches were plastered and painted ...1 a way to resemble carved decoration ...nd stonework. The Abbot enforced strict ...enedictine discipline and founded a ...criptorium which later fostered the tal-...nts of Matthew Paris, Walter of Colch-...ster and others in the 13th century.

They started a series of wall paintings of the Crucifixion and scenes from the life of the Virgin on the west faces of the piers. In the following century large fig-ures of saints were painted on the south faces. All the wall paintings were white-washed during the reign of Edward VI and were only uncovered in 1862. The brilliant colours came away as the white-wash was removed.

Left:
The beheading of Alban – from Matthew Paris's *Life of St Alban*. According to legend, the executioner's eyes fell out as his sword struck.

The Changing Face of the Nave

Very early in the 13th century Abbot John de Cella undertook enormous building works at the west end of the church using the newly discovered stone from Totternhoe in Bedfordshire. It was ideal material for carving and for the new style of architecture – the pointed arch, which allowed lighter and more decorative piers to support the roof. However, though John planned the project, work progressed very slowly. Money was short and the nave had to be finished by his successor William of Trumpington in a less extravagant style. Purbeck shafts, unused bases for detached pillars and cut-outs in capitals all indicate plans for a stone vaulted ceiling which had to be abandoned. Times were hard; King John fell out with Pope Innocent III, who placed an Interdict on the Church in England, and without pilgrims' contributions, funds were further reduced. To

make matters worse Hugh de Goldcliff, the master mason, was unscrupulous and deceitful. The religious squabble between King and Pope developed in 1213 to a meeting here of disgruntled noblemen, which in turn led to John's submission and his sealing of Magna Carta in 1215.

In 1323, whilst a service was in progress, a catastrophe occurred. Two of

Left:
An early 15th-century wall painting of King Offa, high up on the east face of the vault in the north presbytery aisle. The caption to the painting affirms that Offa founded the Benedictine monastery in 793.

Right:
The north side of the nave, showing the 11th-century Norman work, made from Roman bricks plastered and painted to resemble stonework. On the west side of the piers is a sequence of 13th-century paintings of the Crucifixion. On the south side are 14th-century paintings of saints. In the foreground, Abbot John de Cella's 12th-century stone reconstruction of the nave ends above Walter of Colchester's painting.

Left:
In 1323, during the abbacy of Hugh of Eversden, five Norman bays on the south side of the nave collapsed. The reconstruction was made in the Decorated style, in Totternhoe clunch, a soft limestone. The movable choir-stalls, by George Pace, were made in 1972.

he Norman pillars on the south of the ave collapsed outwards. Shortly after- vards the roof of this part of the nave fell 1. Rebuilding was started slowly by bbot Hugh of Eversden. His successor, ichard of Wallingford, continued the vork even more slowly because he was ngrossed in the design of an intricate stronomical clock. The rebuilding was nally completed in 1345 during the bbacy of Michael of Mentmore.

Compare here the more sophisticated arved decoration in the triforium with e simplicity of the Early English work t the west end.

Right: ⑬
The face of Henry Wy, the mason in charge of the 14th-century rebuilding. Other portraits in stone commemorate Abbot Hugh of Eversden, Queen Isabella and King Edward II.

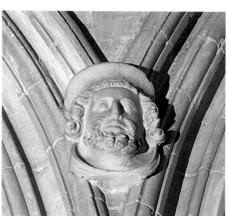

Great Days of the Monastery

In medieval times the choir and presbytery were used exclusively by the monks. For this reason it was customary to screen off the choir from the nave which was frequently used for a variety of secular purposes. The present screen was built about 1360, under Abbot de la Mare, to replace an earlier one damaged in 1323. The two contemporary doors are still used for processional purposes. The screen is a rare survival from monastic times.

The 16th-century Spanish crystal cross behind the altar was presented to the abbey in the 1920s by Canon Glossop in memory of his two sons who died in the First World War. Round the base is a series of small engravings of the Instruments of the Passion, and in the bosses of the cross are prophets reading from their books.

The monastic buildings were mostly on the warm, sheltered south side of the church. The cloisters were in the corner of the nave and the south transept, and the ornate Abbot's doorway shown was on the processional route between the church and the cloisters. Situated in the spandrel above the door is the first-known example of the arms of the abbey in colour.

Nicholas Breakspear, the only Englishman ever to become Pope, had close connections here. He was born about 1100 at nearby Abbots Langley. His father became a monk here, but Nicholas was refused entry as being 'insufficient in learning'. Undaunted, he travelled to France and was accepted by the monastery of St Rufus at Avignon. Later he became Abbot there, then Bishop of Albano, and in 1154 was elected Pope Adrian IV. In spite of his early rejection by the abbey, Adrian granted the Abbot of St Albans permission to assume the mitre, giving him precedence in the Benedictine hierarchy and freedom from the jurisdiction of the Bishop of Lincoln.

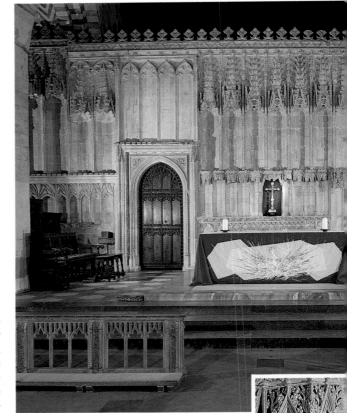

The monastery flourished as a centre of learning and artistic craftsmanship. The scriptorium produced many famous historians, particularly Matthew Paris who wrote the *Chronica Majora* from 1235 until his death in 1259. He was the great chronicler of the 13th century and was the author of the first map of England.

Through the 14th and early 15th centuries the monastery, recognized as the premier Benedictine house in the country, grew in importance and size.

It was ruled by such great abbots as Richard of Wallingford, Thomas de la Mare, John of Wheathampstead and William of Wallingford and had close contact with Oxford University. About 20

dependent houses acknowledged the authority of St Albans Abbey. Its abbots were held in high regard by popes and ruling monarchs. In its heyday there was a community of about 100 monks and some 300 lay helpers. Abbots were busy men. Large estates had to be administered, complex financial affairs controlled, parliamentary attendances made and entertainment of royal or other important personages undertaken.

Left: ⑤
Pope Adrian IV, the only English Pope. Born locally, he was rejected by the abbey, but elected Pope from a French monastery in 1154.

Below: ⑫
The 14th-century Abbot's doorway.

Above: ②
The nave altar and the 14th-century rood screen which divided the monks' choir from the nave. The screen is completely symmetrical. It was damaged at the Reformation, when the statuary was destroyed. The frontal (1978) was designed by Joan Freeman and made by Clarissa Robinson.

Left: ②
The beautifully engraved 16th-century Spanish crystal cross.

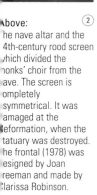

Dissolution

'May the grace of the Holy Spirit be with us'.

TRANSLATION OF PART OF THE INSCRIPTION
ON THE RAMRYGE CHANTRY.

From the early 1520s religious orders were collapsing all over Europe as Renaissance notions began to replace those of medieval Christianity. There were too many religious houses competing for funds and novices, and some houses were lax and corrupt. At St Albans, a civilized atmosphere persisted according to the antiquarian Leland, who was impressed by the scholarly monk who showed him round the abbey library in the 1530s. But the number of monks had dwindled from 100 to 40 by 1529, when Cardinal Wolsey was appointed Abbot, though he remained *in commendam,* that is, an absentee Abbot. He used the income to the benefit of his personal building projects.

King Henry VIII became determined to close all the monasteries and, as part

Right:
Details of delicate fan vaulting on the ceiling of the Ramryge chantry. The chapel was the last piece of masons' work in the church before the dissolution of the monastery and dates from about 1520.

Below:
A pictorial plan by Joan Freeman, located in the north transept, of the medieval monastery when it was a self-contained community. The church and gateway alone remain today. The church kept its white plaster until Victorian times.

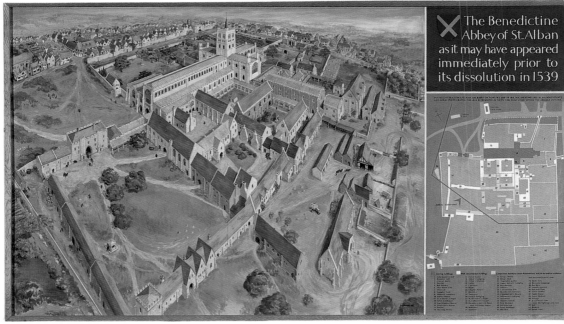

The Benedictine Abbey of St.Alban as it may have appeared immediately prior to its dissolution in 1539

Left: (6)
The Ramryge chantry,
viewed from the
presbytery. It is one of
three chantries in the
cathedral. It
commemorates the
abbacy of the 16th-
century Abbot Ramryge.
Medieval memorials
frequently show a play
on the name being
remembered – a rebus.
There are several
examples on the
external walls here of a
ram bearing the letters
RYGE on its collar.

Right: (6)
Inside the Ramryge
chantry is a stone
transom, visible from the
north aisle, bearing a
ram's head followed by
the letters RYGE, as
though the mason was
emphasizing the fun of
devising his rebus.

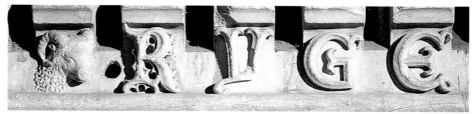

of clever strategies, accused Abbot Catton, Wolsey's successor, of incompetence. Political pressure finally resulted in the abbey's surrender on 5 December 1539. Of the 39 signatures that were on the surrender document, many were in the same hand, which may suggest forgery or a mistaken belief by the monks that they were merely allowing a swift legal transfer from monastery to cathedral, as had happened at Westminster and Peterborough.

Sir Richard Lee, a military engineer, was given the task of destroying the monastic buildings. The materials were sold most profitably for private construction work and road building. All that survived were the church and the great gateway. In 1553 the church was purchased by the townsfolk as their parish church for the sum of £400. This vast acquisition could not be adequately maintained by the limited resources of a small market town and a long slow process of decline and decay began. Throughout the next 300 years, in spite of several efforts at essential repairs, deterioration continued until, by the early 1800s, the only parts still usable for worship were the choir and presbytery.

The Transepts

The north transept is Norman except for the part above the balcony, which is 19th-century. The clock mechanism on the floor by the west wall is a modern representation of Richard of Wallingford's astronomical clock of the early 14th century. Next to it is an altar frontal cupboard carved entirely by ladies, a gift from Canon Woolmore Wigram in 1905. The busts are of Lord Grimthorpe, Archdeacon Grant and Dean Lawrance, all of whom were dominant personalities in the restoration. The tomb effigy of the first Bishop, Thomas Legh Claughton

Cor mundum in me crea Deus.
'Make a clean heart in me, oh God.'

FROM ROBERT BEAUNER'S BRASS (1470) IN THE PRESBYTERY

(1877–90), is by Forsyth. In a window on the east side are the 14th-century coats of arms of Edward III and three of his sons. The altar is dedicated to the 'Persecuted Church', linking the persecution of Alban with the victims of modern oppression. On the east wall is a 15th-century mural of Doubting Thomas, discovered under whitewash in 1846.

Left:
The north transept, showing Lord Grimthorpe's Victorian window. In 1989, to celebrate their 100th birthday, Laporte Industries funded its reglazing, designed by Alan Younger. Norman arches support the finest 11th-century tower in the country.

Left: (10)
The south wall of the south transept was completely reconstructed by Lord Grimthorpe in the 1880s. The Norman arcading beneath the lancet windows was re-sited by him from the Norman slype (the passageway to the Chapter House). The Michael Stair (1986) is a memorial to Bishop Michael Gresford-Jones (1950–70) and provides the choir and clergy with an impressive entrance from the vestries in the Chapter House.

Left: (10)
The ringed baluster shafts in the triforium of both transepts are of Saxon origin, turned on a lathe. The cushion capitals are Norman. Roman tiles visible in the crescents above the balusters in the south transept are a clear reminder that Paul of Caen used the abandoned Roman city of Verulamium for building materials.

The lancet windows in the south wall are Grimthorpe's work and the arms of subscribers are displayed in the glass. The early medieval bell over the gallery was most probably the Sanctus bell. This served as the school bell for 300 years while a school was located in the Lady Chapel. Both the arcading over the gallery and the doorway beneath are 11th-century; both have been relocated from the slype, the passageway to the Chapter House. The pointed windows on the west side of the south transept were inserted when the cloisters were rebuilt in the 14th century after the collapse of the nave pillars. The alcove in the west wall used to be an entrance and now contains dole cupboards (a 17th-century bequest) and wooden bosses from the Lady Chapel ceiling which were removed in Grimthorpe's 19th-century restoration.

Right: ⑤
The presbytery in 1850 showing the high altar screen. Originally constructed *c*.1484 to exclude pilgrims to the shrine from the choir, its statues were destroyed after the Dissolution.

Far right: ⑤
The high altar screen today. The present statues were installed by Lord Aldenham in the 1890s.

Below left: ⑤
The presbytery ceiling.was made in wood in the 13th century – the earliest painted wooden vaulted ceiling, repainted in the 15th century. Shields were added during 17th-century restoration.

Below centre: ⑤
The reredos, a bas-relief sculpture of marble and paua shell by Sir Alfred Gilbert.

The Tower and Presbytery

In the 17th century the choir ceiling was overpainted in a mediocre fashion. In 1875, during essential strengthening, it was found that the panels were removable. On close examination, early medieval paintings were discovered under the 17th-century work. When this was removed, the original painting was revealed. At this time a charge of 6d. was levied on those visitors who wished to pass through from the nave to the east end of the church. It was money from this fund which paid for the restoration of the 66 panels.

The tower is the oldest of this country's great cathedral towers. Its walls are seven feet thick and are built of Roman tiles which were already about 800 years old when the Normans used them in 1080. In the 1330s the tower was twice struck by lightning. The abbot of the day

Above: ④
The tower ceiling, 102 feet (31m) above ground level. Painted in the 15th century to commemorate the first battle of the Wars of the Roses, fought in St Albans in 1455. Due to deterioration it was copied on a false ceiling 1951–2.

Left: ③
The choir ceiling, possibly dated 1368–76 with later modifications to the sixth row.

placed a papal seal bearing the *Agnus Dei* on the highest point for protection – alas ineffectively. Extensive reconstruction of a more practical nature was necessary in 1870. The north-east pier was bursting under pressure because of 14th-century alterations, and the south corner had been undermined during the Dissolution. The whole tower was threatened with imminent collapse.

Immediately above the tower ceiling is the ringing chamber, and yet higher still the only ring of 12 bells in the county. Of these, four date from 1699 and the four smallest were added to the existing eight to celebrate the Silver Jubilee of H M King George V in 1935.

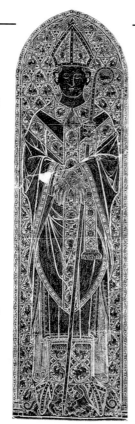

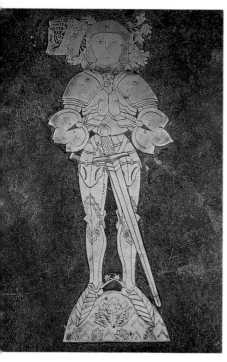

Auxilium meum a Domino, qui fecit caelum et terram.
'My help cometh from the Lord,
who made heaven and earth.'

PSALM 121, SUNG IN LATIN AT THE REBURIAL OF THE ABBOTS
UNDER THE KINDERSLEY SLATE, 21 NOVEMBER 1979.

The presbytery floor is tiled with 19th-century Minton reproductions of tiles used originally in the 11th-century Chapter House, discovered in earlier excavations. Several abbots were buried under this floor. Their fine memorial brasses have been plundered and only the indents remain. The vaulted ceiling, originally planned in stone, was actually made in wood in the 13th century because of the cost. It was repainted in the 15th century by Abbot John of Wheathampstead.

HERE REST THE MORTAL REMAINS ☉ ABBOTS FROM 1077 To 1401 · PAUL OF CAEN · RICHARD d'ALBINI · GEOFFREY ☉ GORRON · RALPH GUBION · ROBERT of GORRON · SIMON · WARIN ☉ CAMBRIDGE · JOHN de CELLA · WILLIAM OF TRUMPINGToN · JOHN ☉ HERTFORD · JOHN de la MOOTE

And also of RoBERT the CHAMBER father of Pope Adrian IV · ADAM THE CELLARER Prior ADAM WITTENHAM · ADAM ROUS Surgeon to Edward III

REMOVED in 1978 from The CHAPTER HOUSE

SEEK FIRST THE KINGDOM OF GOD

The Chapel of St Alban

The Chapel of St Alban was the focus of religious observance for both the local community and the visiting pilgrims. The relics of the saint were contained in a magnificent silver-gilt reliquary which was heavily encrusted with jewels. This was placed on a large, elaborately built pedestal. The relics had a reputation for their miraculous healing powers and offerings were made here by hopeful pilgrims. All were expected to give, whether rich or poor. Many would purchase the pilgrim badge of St Alban.

At the Dissolution, the reliquary was seized by the Crown and the pedestal was destroyed to be used as common building material. At this time the Lady Chapel was walled off from the main body of the church. When this was removed in the 1870s, the fragments of the pedestal were recovered and it was rebuilt. In 1991, modern technology and materials allowed an improved reconstruction to be carried out.

Right: ⑦
The martyrdom of St Alban with angels swinging censers at the west end of his shrine.

Below: ⑦
The Chapel of St Alban, with the shrine in the centre and the watching loft to the north.

Right:
John of Wheathampstead, Abbot 1420–40 and 1451–65, from the Golden Book of St Albans.

Right: (7)
The martyrdom of St Alban carved in the centre of the oak beam of the watching loft.

charge of the shrine) on the activity round the shrine itself. Monastic watchers could also see the length of the north aisle, from which direction the stream of pilgrims would be approaching.

On the south side is the only royal tomb in the church, the chantry of Humphrey, Duke of Gloucester, youngest brother of King Henry V. He and Abbot John of Wheathampstead met as scholars at Oxford and remained lifelong friends.

On the south of the chantry are 17 statues of kings, the only surviving pre-Reformation figures in the church. Beneath is a 13th-century wrought-iron screen which kept pilgrims at a respectful distance from the shrine.

As a result of the large number of pilgrimages made to the saint's shrine, his chapel would, from time to time, become congested and a considerable amount of offerings would build up. There was also the immensely valuable reliquary casket and other relics to protect. So the watching chamber was built about 1400. From its upper storey a watch could be kept by the *custos feretri* (the monk in

Above: (8)
Humphrey, Duke of Gloucester's monument, 1446, built over the vault containing his remains but not obstructing the pilgrims' view of the shrine.

Below:
The Chapel of St Alban, seen from the east.

Left: (7)
St William of York, painted about 1330; most of the original colouring is intact, preserved by the 16th-century construction of a wall. The cross staff has been painted over a crozier. The arms on the shield are those of the Fitzherbert family in the 14th century.

The Lady Chapel

The 11th-century church terminated in an apse at the east end of the Chapel of St Alban, with two smaller apses at the ends of the aisles. Thus there was no direct access from north to south aisles. As processions began to be introduced into monastic ritual this layout became unsatisfactory.

Towards the end of the 13th century the veneration of the Virgin was becoming important to Christians and special chapels were being built in her name at the east end of some large churches. In 1257 the east end of the church was becoming unsound. The necessary reconstruction provided the opportunity to

Right:
For 300 years the Lady Chapel was walled off from the main body of the church, and used as a boys' school. A public pathway was actually driven through between the two parts. Here we see the entrance to the passageway, viewed from the south.

make a processional route round the Chapel of St Alban and also to build a special chapel dedicated to the Virgin Mary, completed during the abbacy of Hugh of Eversden about 1320.

When the church was taken over by the townspeople in 1553 for use as their parish church it was walled off from the main body and a public passageway was driven through from north to south. The chapel was occupied by the boys of the grammar school for the next 300 years. When the school was transferred to the great gateway in 1871 and the public passageway was closed the local people were very angry and started a riot. The chapel was found to be in a very poor condition and, in view of its dedication, a committee of local influential ladies was formed to raise funds for its restoration, with little result. Lord Grimthorpe completed the fund and restored the chapel to its present condition. The marble flooring, the arcading round the walls and the stone vaulting are all part of this restoration. The stone vault is a

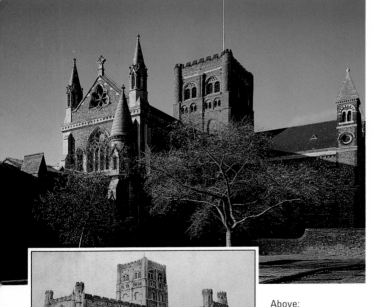

Above:
The cathedral today, set prominently on its hill site where Alban's martyrdom took place early in the 3rd century.

Left:
An earlier view, before the major Victorian restoration.

Left:
Looking east in the
Lady Chapel. Completed
about 1320 as the final
reordering of the east
end of the church, this
attractive extension was
sadly neglected when,
after the Dissolution, it
housed a school. It was
restored to its present
state by Lord
Grimthorpe. The
furniture was given by
the Kent family
(1948–53).

opy of the original timber one, and
ome of the bosses are retained in the
lcove in the south transept. The
vindow jambs with the ball flower decoration and the little figures on the mul-
ions are original 14th-century work.

At the south end of the retrochoir –
he vestibule of the Lady Chapel – is the
Chapel of the Four Tapers. In 1931 the
Mothers' Union of the diocese dedicated
his chapel to their use and inserted an
ltar. At the north end is the Chapel of
St Michael, restored in 1927.

Right:
The Lady Chapel as a
schoolroom, showing
the abbey cope table. In
1871 Sir George Gilbert
Scott complained
bitterly that he found the
chapel 'a mere ruin;
excepting the roof, it is
rudely repaired with
brick and has suffered
from deliberate
mutilation.'

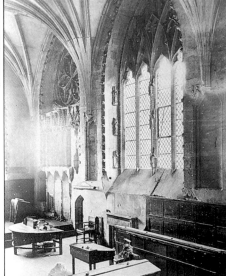

Victorian Restoration

From time to time after the Dissolution minor repairs to the abbey were carried out but, as an early 18th-century historian of Hertfordshire sadly remarked, 'This noble Fabrick hath, since it became a Parish Church, wanted its Abbots Zeal and Purse too for repairs.' An epoch of *laisser tomber* had begun.

Below:
The west front. This was redesigned and largely rebuilt in Victorian Gothic style by Lord Grimthorpe in the 1880s.

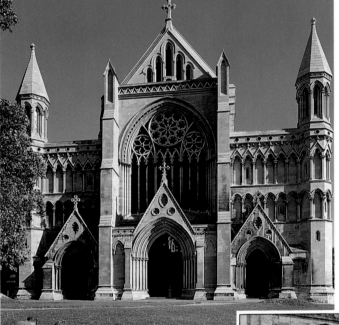

In 1832 a part of the wall on the south side of the nave fell through the roof of the south aisle. Clearly a state of crisis had been reached. Serious efforts at restoration were made by L. N. Cottingham, but these were curtailed by lack of sufficient funds.

In 1856 Sir George Gilbert Scott was appointed Architect and a restoration committee was formed. Lord Grimthorpe, a very rich man (who had lately designed

the clock mechanism of Big Ben), was present at a public meeting called to raise funds. A barrister by profession, he was also an opinionated amateur architect. It was generally assumed that the committee's decisions would be endorsed by Lord Grimthorpe. However, it became quite apparent in the next few years that he intended to control the entire restoration project himself.

Much of the money raised by the restoration committee was spent on buying back the land immediately adjacent to the church, which had long been in private hands. At first Lord Grimthorpe remained on reasonably good terms with Sir George Gilbert Scott, who directed the restoration of the tower in 1870. This work reflected great credit on John Chapple, the clerk of works. While in a service he heard an ominous crack from the tower. He found that the north-east corner was moving. Scott was ill in bed so Chapple and his men worked four days and nights with shoring and brickwork to halt the movement and thus save the tower. When the condition of the south side of the nave became dangerous, Grimthorpe became highly critical of Scott's poor design for the positioning of jacks to restore the leaning

Left::
The medieval west front had an attractive 15th-century window and splendid doors, but in 1880 was found to be in a very bad state of repair, requiring extensive treatment.

Right:
The body of the church from the south-west at the time of Lord Grimthorpe's restoration

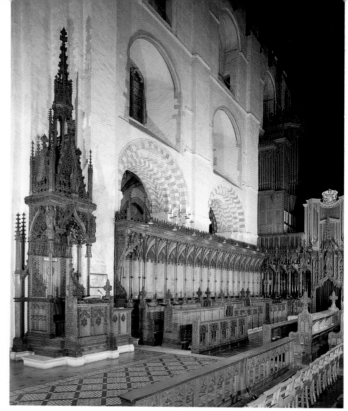

wall to an upright position. Grimthorpe himself designed a different system using newly-developed hydraulic jacks and then proceeded to carry it out, successfully. Full of self-confidence he then prevailed in his controversial plan to alter the pitch of the nave roof, which changed the appearance of the church.

In 1877 the Diocese of St Albans was created, and at last the church became a

Above left:
Lord Grimthorpe, a controversial and forceful character, the driving force behind the Victorian restoration.

Above right: ③
The Bishop's throne and the choir-stalls (1903) were designed by J. O. Scott.

cathedral, with Thomas Legh Claughton as the first Bishop. The elevated status of the church helped to generate more funds for the restoration but the scale and urgency of the repairs presented a huge problem. To the already elderly Bishop, perhaps hoping for a quiet life in his twilight years, the solution probably looked simple. Here was Lord Grimthorpe offering large sums of money needed to repair the dilapidated building.

When Sir George Gilbert Scott died the next year, Lord Grimthorpe wrote himself a Faculty to restore the church at his own expense. He submitted it to the Bishop in 1880 and, despite the misgivings of many, the Bishop granted it. This gave Lord Grimthorpe licence to make any alterations to the church that he considered fit. He replaced the beautiful west front with one of his own design, and completely changed the end windows in the north and south transepts, causing much controversy both locally and nationally. Indeed, it was the activities of 'restorers' of his kind which caused Parliament to pass the Ancient Monuments Protection Act in 1882.

The Lords go to Law

During the 1890s the high altar screen was restored by Lord Aldenham, a man with High Church leanings. He engaged the services of the architect Sir Arthur Blomfield, with Harry Hems as mason. They designed and carved statues to replace those destroyed during the Reformation. Lord Aldenham felt uncertain about the identity of all the original statues, and chose to replace them with figures pertaining to the history of the abbey, together with the customary saints. But when it became clear to the ultra-protestant Lord Grimthorpe that a crucifix was to dominate the scheme, he objected violently. He proposed instead to insert in the cruciform space the statues of Queen Elizabeth I, Queen Victoria, Cardinal Wolsey and the Bishop. Lord Aldenham and the Bishop were appalled. An expensive court case ensued, which Lord Aldenham won and the crucifix was inserted, to general acclaim. (At Winchester Cathedral, where Bodley had been similarly restoring their high altar screen, no such controversy had arisen.) There was considerable acrimony generated. Aldenham's men frequently fell foul of Grimthorpe's resident team at the cathedral. Their private nickname for Grimthorpe, who had been born Edmund

Below: ①
Lord Grimthorpe's draught-excluding west doors were replaced in 1988 by glass doors engraved by David Peace. The glass windows above them were engraved by Sally Scott (1988).

Beckett, was 'Pope Edmund à Becket'. Despite this Lord Aldenham managed afterwards to maintain a friendly relationship with Lord Grimthorpe. No doubt he recognized, as we do today, that although Lord Grimthorpe destroyed much of the late medieval architecture, he also spent a great deal of money making many sound repairs and undoubtedly saved the church from falling into ruin. Clearly Grimthorpe

Above: (9)

bove: (9)
he 17th-century parish
oor box and wooden
gure begging alms. The
riginal figure is now in
e treasury.

bove:
he abbey church from
he south-east before
e 19th-century
estoration. It then had
s Norman turrets and
Hertfordshire spike' on
e tower.

ight:
similar view today,
howing the effects of
estoration.

relished con-troversy; Lord Aldenham and the clergy equally clearly did not.

The only lasting disappointment to Lord Aldenham was Sir Alfred Gilbert's bas-relief sculpture on the reredos, which was never finished, as the sculptor's royal commissions had to take prece-dence. The subject of the sculpture is the Resurrection. The figure of Christ is rising from the tomb: above, the hands of God remove his crown of thorns whilst two angels remove the cross and the earth – symbolic of his burdens. The figures are made of marble and the iridescent angels'

wings of paua shells from New Zealand.

The stained glass windows in the cathedral date from Victorian times. A few fragments of medieval glass remain and are set into windows in the east wall of the north transept. There are several attractive 19th-century windows in the Lady Chapel. The east window was given by the Corporation of the City of London. The western window in the south side commemorates the 50th wedding anniversary of Lord and Lady Grim-thorpe, and the south-east window above the sedilia was given by the livery com-panies of London – their armorial bear-ings can be seen in the stained glass.

The great west window was reglazed by Sir Ninian Comper in 1924. It is the diocesan war memorial for the 1914–18 war and shows soldier saints, together with the insignia of the Allies.

The very latest addition is Alan Younger's rose window in the north transept, commemorating the centenary of Laporte Industries of Luton.

The Chapter House

The Chapter House was the administrative centre of the medieval monastery. The original building at St Albans was large enough to accommodate the whole community of monks, and they would meet daily under their abbot to deal with matters of discipline, management and finance. One practice which they invariably observed was the reading of a chapter of the Benedictine Rule. This is how the building came to be known as the Chapter House. After the Dissolution, the major function of the beautiful 15th-century building no longer existed, and in about 1550 Sir Richard Lee set to work pulling it down. An architectural treasure was destroyed and sold off as builders' rubble.

Right:
The problems of pollution: a lion's head ornament, on the south side of the nave at parapet level, damaged by acid rain. These heads have to be replaced when necessary.

Below:
South-east view of the Chapter House, a multi-purpose building, designed by William Whitfield & Partners, 1982. It is the first modern building to be placed beside a medieval church.

Left:
A sculpture (1979) of Robert Runcie, then Bishop of St Albans, later Archbishop of Canterbury, 1980–91.

Left:
A sculpture (1979) of Peter Moore, the Dean, who inspired the building of the Chapter House in 1982.

In spite of the radical change in the manner in which the church was then used – not as a monastery but as a parish church – extra space was always needed. With a modern community based society, parish activities became increasingly cramped and overflowed into nearby buildings. Towards the end of 1977 the Dean, The Very Revd Dr Peter Moore, called a Parish Meeting and presented his vision of a new Chapter House. A research committee proved this to be feasible; thus began the long and arduous process of fund-raising, planning and translating a vision into reality.

'This is none other but the House of God, and this is the Gate of Heaven.'

JOHN CHAPPLE,
CLERK OF THE WORKS FOR THE VICTORIAN RESTORATION.

Left: ⑪
Upstairs in the Chapter House is a modern theological library.

The location finally chosen was on the south side of the cathedral where previous chapter houses had stood. A provision in the planning permission required that, before building could begin, a thorough archaeological examination of the area be made. On 29 May 1978, Professor Martin Biddle FSA and Magister Birthe Kjolbye-Biddle FSA began to excavate the site. Many interesting finds came to light, including the remains of early abbots and monks. After careful study, these were removed to a designated new burial place in the presbytery.

After the excavation was finished, building began. To the cathedral users, ever pressed for space, progress seemed slow, but eventually the new Chapter House was finished, and opened by HM Queen Elizabeth II in 1982.

The architect, William Whitfield, took great care to design a building which not only provided the facilities so badly needed but was also compatible with the venerable Norman church. Handmade red bricks were specifically designed to complement the Roman tiles of the abbey. The new Chapter House has an apsidal east end, like the original Chapter House built by Paul de Caen in 1077.

The building houses a song school, offices, counselling rooms and a modern theological library. On the library level there is an architecturally interesting bridge from the vestry to a gallery in the south transept, and from this a memorial staircase leads to the body of the church. The whole unit provides versatile facilities for the congregation and visitors. There is a shop, a popular refectory, an information desk and toilets. The spacious crypt is well suited as a meeting place for numerous activities.

Above: ⑪
The refectory, on the ground floor of the Chapter House. A popular venue for visitors and local townspeople.

Music is of paramount importance in the cathedral today, as it was in the past. Records show that an organ existed in the monastery in 1302 and vocal music evidently flourished too, as the Bishop of Durham complained that a 'singing boy' was enticed from Durham to St Albans early in the 15th century. Today, the local boys and men sing splendidly and need no such augmentation from afar.

The Church Today

The cathedral is often used for concerts and in 1962 the International Organ Festival was inaugurated – a biennial event which attracts the most distinguished musicians.

This cathedral is a parish church so the Dean is also its Rector. He is assisted by canons and other clergy, supported by the virgers. Close contact is maintained with Lutherans, Nonconformists and Roman Catholics, some of whom hold their own services here. There is a large congregation which provides voluntary helpers in the refectory, the shop and the bookstall and who serve as bellringers, guides, watchers, welcomers, youth leaders, members of the flower guild and the textile group. Helpers are also provided by other parishes of the diocese as over 400 people are needed in the day-to-day running of the church. A number of special projects – like the provision of glass doors at the west end – are funded by the Fraternity of the Friends of St Albans Abbey. The Fraternity was originally

Above:
The Gospel being sung before the high altar at Solemn Eucharist.

Below:
The cathedral choir at the steps of the presbytery.

founded by Abbot John of Wheatham stead in the 15th century.

The lively education centre works conjunction with the schools of the dicese to provide various courses and visit specially tailored to the needs of th National Curriculum. Activities rang from craft sessions for young childre through to advanced technical and arch tectural sessions for GCSE students. Th education centre has twice won the San ford Award for its 'outstanding contribution to heritage education'.

Today the visitor will find the churc in vigorous health with all the bustle daily life and congregational worship indeed a chapel has had to be set asic for private prayer and meditation. Th services which include traditional proce sions keep us in touch with our past particularly at St Albanstide, on 22 Jun when many bring offerings of roses the shrine of Alban, the 'Rose of Ma tyrs'. Easter brings young visitors in the thousands from far and near to a weel end of youth pilgrimage. At Christma children celebrate with a Christingle se vice, a festival which originates in th Moravian church and reminds us of ou links with Christians of all lands, concer trating our minds on loving and givin at home and abroad.